AUTUMN

AN ALPHABET ACROSTIC

AUTUMN

AN ALPHABET ACROSTIC

by Steven Schnur
Illustrated by Leslie Evans

CLARION BOOKS
New York

Clarion Books
a Houghton Mifflin Company imprint
215 Park Avenue South, New York, NY 10003
Text copyright © 1997 by Steven Schnur
Illustrations copyright © 1997 by Leslie Evans

Illustrations executed in hand-colored linoleum cut blocks.
Text is 19/25-point Galliard.
Book design by Carol Goldenberg.

For information about permission to reproduce selections from this book,
write to Permissions, Houghton Mifflin Company, 215 Park Avenue South,
New York, NY 10003.

Printed in Singapore.

Library of Congress Cataloging-in-Publication Data
Schnur, Steven.
Autumn: an alphabet acrostic / by Steven Schnur : illustrated by Leslie Evans.
p.   cm
Summary: Describes the autumn season, with its animals, rain, cold winds, and harvested food.
When read vertically, the first letters of the lines of text spell related words arranged alphabetically,
from "acorn" to "zero."
ISBN: 0-395-77043-2
1. Autumn—Juvenile literature. 2. Acrostics—Juvenile literature [1. Autumn. 2. Acrostics.
3. Alphabet.] I. Evans, Leslie, ill. II. Title.
QB637.7.S36 1997
793.73—dc21   [E] 9650219
CIP   AC

TWP 10 9 8 7 6

For Melanie Amariglio, in loving memory
—S.S.

To my parents, Shirley and Gomer Evans
—L.E.

A single seed
C an feed a squirrel
O r grow into a giant oak that
R ains down new
N uts every autumn.

Bats
And owls
Roost among empty
Nests.

Come October,
Only the harvested stalks
Remain in the fields as the
Nights turn frosty.

Day ends early
And night lingers; a cold
Rain falls as we
Kindle the fireplace.

Every plant,
Animal and
Rock, the air itself,
Turns slowly under
Heaven.

From the window the
Rows of
Orange pumpkins
Seem clothed in
Thin white shawls.

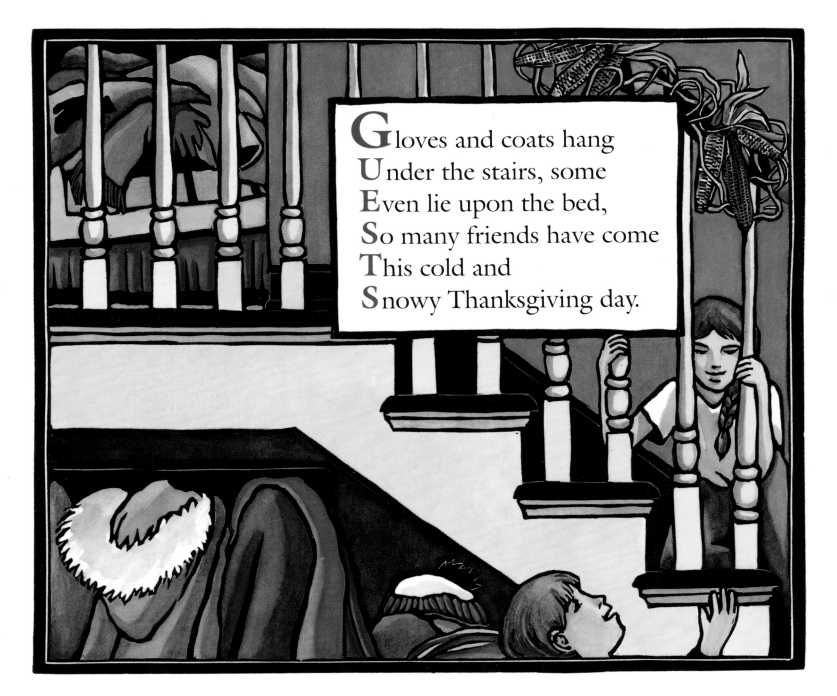

Gloves and coats hang
Under the stairs, some
Even lie upon the bed,
So many friends have come
This cold and
Snowy Thanksgiving day.

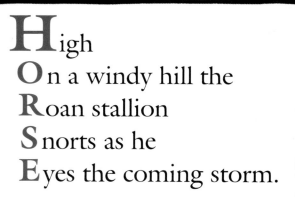

High
On a windy hill the
Roan stallion
Snorts as he
Eyes the coming storm.

In the north
Cones of
Ice
Cling
Like whiskers to the
Eaves.

Jars of freshly made
Applesauce, jelly, and
Marmalade sit gleaming on the kitchen shelf.

Keeping hands busy, the
Needles click and
Inch by inch a
Thick wool shawl appears.

Little remains on
Each maple, oak, and
Aspen tree; even the grape
Vines have shriveled,
Ending another green
Season.

Moving quickly
Over the breadboard and
Under the toaster, the intruder
Stuffs both cheeks with crumbs to
Eat later hiding in the wall.

Now cold winds come down
Out of Canada and the
Rain
Turns to
Hail and then to snow.

On sky-dark
Wings this hunter needs no
Light to find its prey.

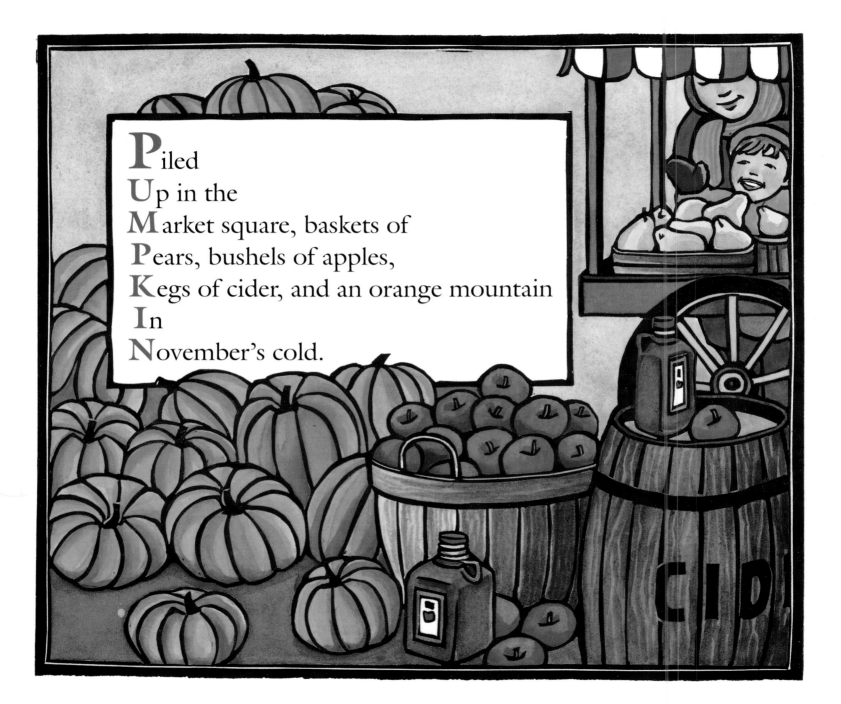

Piled
Up in the
Market square, baskets of
Pears, bushels of apples,
Kegs of cider, and an orange mountain
In
November's cold.

Quilts lie heaped
Upon the beds this
Icy
Evening
To keep us warm.

Red apples in bushel baskets
In the cellar, soon to become
Pies or applesauce or shined and
Eaten on the way to school.

Stillness
Now
Over all the cold
White world.

The distant
Rumble of wheels
And the mournful wail of a whistle
In the
Night.

Up beyond the
Night sky, an
Indigo darkness like
Velvet
Embraces the farthest
Reaches of the mind,
Sun, moon, stars,
Everything.

Venus glows brightly

In the western sky, beyond the

Lights and

Laughter

And the busy

Going to and fro of

Everyone in town.

Winter is almost **H**ere and just **I**n **T**ime. There's snow **E**verywhere.

XII, the twelfth month of the
Year, when the
Last leaf has fallen and
Every plant stem withers or rests until
May.

Yesterday December
Ended. Today more than just
Another month begins.
Rejoice!